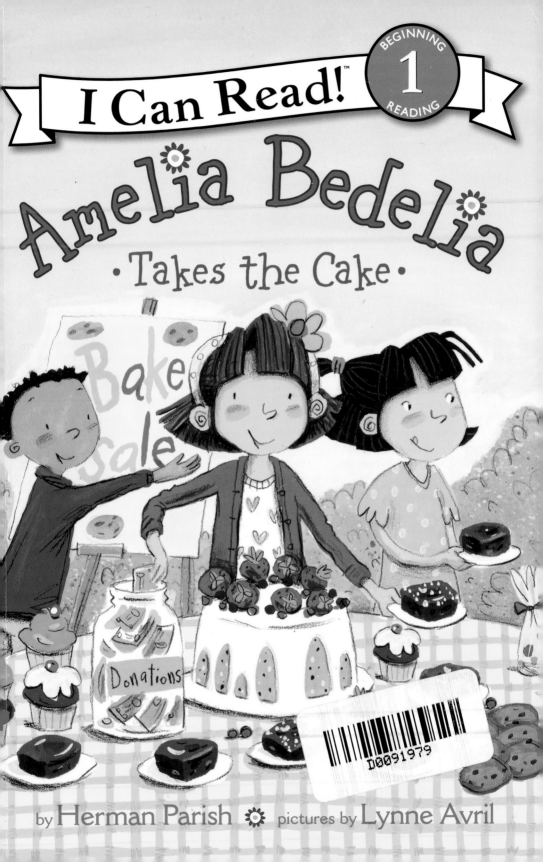

Amelia Bedelia
·Takes the Cake·

Bake Sale

Donations

D0091979

by **Herman Parish** ❁ pictures by **Lynne Avril**

HOORAY!

_____

can read this book!

www.harpercollinschildrens.com
BOOK NEWS, GAMES, CONTESTS, AND MORE

USA $3.99 / $4.99 CAN
ISBN 978-0-06-233430-5

50399

17 05

S

Dear Parent:
Your child's love of reading starts here!

Every child learns to read in a different way and at his or her own speed. Some go back and forth between reading levels and read favorite books again and again. Others read through each level in order. You can help your young reader improve and become more confident by encouraging his or her own interests and abilities. From books your child reads with you to the first books he or she reads alone, there are I Can Read Books for every stage of reading:

SHARED READING
Basic language, word repetition, and whimsical illustrations, ideal for sharing with your emergent reader

BEGINNING READING
Short sentences, familiar words, and simple concepts for children eager to read on their own

READING WITH HELP
Engaging stories, longer sentences, and language play for developing readers

READING ALONE
Complex plots, challenging vocabulary, and high-interest topics for the independent reader

ADVANCED READING
Short paragraphs, chapters, and exciting themes for the perfect bridge to chapter books

I Can Read Books have introduced children to the joy of reading since 1957. Featuring award-winning authors and illustrators and a fabulous cast of beloved characters, I Can Read Books set the standard for beginning readers.

A lifetime of discovery begins with the magical words "I Can Read!"

Visit www.icanread.com for information
on enriching your child's reading experience.

For Debbie & Jesse, a couple of cake takers!
—H. P.

To Tanja for all her generosity of time, know-how,
and spirit. Many thanks!
—L. A.

Gouache and black pencil were used to prepare the full-color art.

I Can Read Book® is a trademark of HarperCollins Publishers.

Amelia Bedelia is a registered trademark of Peppermint Partners, LLC.

Amelia Bedelia Takes the Cake. Text copyright © 2016 by Herman S. Parish III. Illustrations copyright © 2016 by Lynne Avril. All rights reserved. No part of this book may be used or reproduced in any manner whatsoever without written permission except in the case of brief quotations embodied in critical articles and reviews. Printed in the U.S.A. For information address HarperCollins Children's Books, a division of HarperCollins Publishers, 195 Broadway, New York, NY 10007.

www.icanread.com

Library of Congress Cataloging-in-Publication Data is available.

ISBN 978-0-06-233431-2 (hardback)—ISBN 978-0-06-233430-5 (pbk)

17 18 19 20 LSCC 10 9 8 7 6 5 First Edition

Greenwillow Books

I Can Read!™

BEGINNING 1 READING

Amelia Bedelia
·Takes the Cake·

by Herman Parish ✿ pictures by Lynne Avril

Greenwillow Books, *An Imprint of* HarperCollins*Publishers*

Amelia Bedelia and her classmates
were having a bake sale.
The bake sale would raise money
to help the library at their school
buy new books.

"My mom helped me make an angel food cake," said Angel.

Amelia Bedelia thought everything Angel ate was angel food.

"I made chocolate chip brownies," said Chip.

"Of course," said Amelia Bedelia. She was excited to share the super chewy brownies she had made.

Just then, Wade arrived with brownies.

So did Dawn and Holly and Heather.

Teddy and Clay brought brownies, too.

So did the rest of the class.

"Guys," said Chip.

"This is a bake sale,

not a brownie festival."

Miss Edwards, their teacher,

arrived with a big glass jar

to hold the money

from the sale.

"My goodness," she said.

"I've seen lots of mix-ups,

but this takes the cake."

"Please do not take our cake!"

said Amelia Bedelia.

"It's the only one we've got."

"Don't worry. I'll buy the cake,"

said Miss Edwards.

"I have plans for it!"

"Thank you," said Angel.

She put the money from Miss Edwards

in the big glass jar.

"Go ahead and get set up,"

said Miss Edwards.

"I'll be back."

Amelia Bedelia and her classmates
stared at stacks of brownies.

"Maybe we should put out a few
at a time," said Dawn.

Clay and Teddy gave her idea a try.

"That looks weird," said Wade.

"We did a lot of baking,

but I do not think we will sell a lot."

"I know," said Amelia Bedelia.

"Let's put them

all out at once!"

The brownies
were all square.

They were all about the same size.

But the light, cakey
ones were tall.

The dark, chewy
ones were short.

Some had flaky tops.

Others were smooth and flat.

Teddy had put icing on his batch.

Holly had dusted her batch
with powdered sugar.

The bakers stood back

to admire their work.

"That looks amazing," said Penny.

"I've never seen so much chocolate."

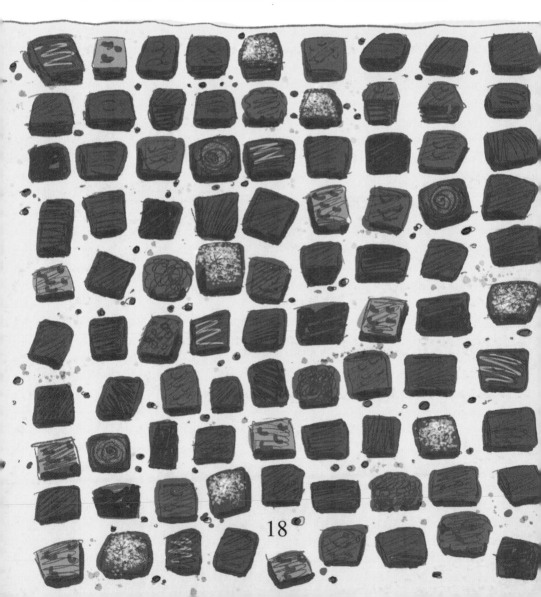

18

"It's cool," said Skip.
"They are the same
but also not the same."

Cliff squinted his eyes.

"Too bad we can't make

one big brownie!" he said.

"We could set a world record

for biggest brownie."

Amelia Bedelia squinted her eyes.

She could see what Cliff saw.

She also saw something else.

She began moving brownies

here and there
and everywhere.

Amelia Bedelia stood back
to admire her work.
"Now that is one big brown 'E'!"
she said.

Everyone laughed and cheered.

"That is amazing," said Angel.

"We need new signs," said Clay.

Everyone got to work.

Soon, kids from other classes
came to the bake sale.

Parents and babysitters
stopped by.

So did teachers
and bus drivers.

The principal and the school nurse
visited, too.

Everyone wanted a taste of
the biggest brown "E" in town.

"Wow!" said Miss Edwards.

"I've been to many bake sales,

but this really does take the cake!"

"No, you bought the cake!"

said Amelia Bedelia.

"I did," said Miss Edwards.

"I thought the best bakers in town

might like a snack

when their work was done."

"Thanks, Miss Edwards," said Angel.

She was trying to smile.

"I do like angel food cakes,

but I really wanted to try a brownie.

We sold out before I got a taste."

"Well, you can't have your cake

and eat it, too," said Miss Edwards.

"What good is having a cake

if you can't eat it?"

said Amelia Bedelia.

"Good point," said Miss Edwards.

She cut the cake into even slices.

Everyone enjoyed the treat.

This time, they could

have their cake

and eat it, too!